ABOUT THE AUTHOR

Neil Ardley has written a number of innovative nonfiction books for children, including *The Eyewitness Guide to Music*. He also worked closely with David Macaulay on *The Way Things Work*. In addition to being a well-known author in the fields of science, technology, and music, he is an accomplished musician who composes and performs both jazz and electronic music. He lives in Derbyshire, England, with his wife and daughter.

Project Editor Linda Martin
Art Editor Peter Bailey
Designer Mark Regardsoe
Photography Pete Gardner
Created by Dorling Kindersley Limited, London

Library of Congress Cataloging-in-Publication Data
Ardley, Neil.
The science book of things that grow/Neil Ardley.—1st U.S. ed.
p. cm.
"Gulliver books."
Summary: Simple experiments explain plant growth.
ISBN 0-15-200586-2
1. Growth (Plants)—Experiments—Juvenile literature. [1. Growth (Plants)—Experiments. 2. Experiments.] I. Title.
QK731.A73 1991
581.3'1'078—dc20   90-48097

Printed in Belgium by Proost
First U.S. edition 1991
A B C D E

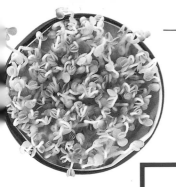

THE SCIENCE BOOK OF THINGS THAT GROW

Neil Ardley

HBJ

Gulliver Books

Harcourt Brace Jovanovich, Publishers

San Diego   New York   London

What is growth?

All living things need food to grow. The food we eat comes from plants or from animals that eat plants. But what do plants eat? Green plants make their own food from air, water, and sunlight. Plants use this food to grow stems and leaves and sometimes flowers and fruits. Trees that start life as tiny seeds can grow to thousands of times their original size.

A world of life

All life on earth depends on the growth of plants. Plants produce much of the oxygen in the atmosphere that people and animals need to live.

Water your plants

Plants need water to live. Without water they will stop growing and die.

Useful plants

This boy's sweatshirt is made of cotton, which comes from a tropical plant. The pages of the book he is reading are made from wood fibers from trees.

Good food

Fruits and vegetables are just some of the wholesome foods that come from plants. Breads, sugars, and cereals are also made from plants.

Greatest growth

Sequoia trees are the tallest living things in the world. They can grow as high as 110 meters (361 feet). As they grow from seeds, these trees increase their weight about a million million times!

⚠ This is a warning symbol. It appears within an experiment next to a step that requires caution. When you see this symbol, ask an adult for help.

Be a safe scientist
Follow all the instructions carefully and always use caution, especially with glass, scissors, matches, and disinfectant.

If you do not want to waste the seedlings you have grown, you can plant them in pots or in a garden.

Starting to grow

How do plants grow? Many grow from seeds formed by parent plants. A bean is the seed of a bean plant. See what happens when a bean begins to grow, or "germinates."

You will need:

Water

Paper towels

Tall glass jar

Bowl of water

Bean seeds

1 Soak a few beans in water overnight.

2 Roll up several paper towels. Put them into the jar.

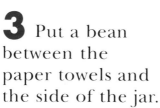

3 Put a bean between the paper towels and the side of the jar.

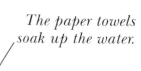

The paper towels soak up the water.

4 Add enough water to the jar to moisten the paper towels. Put the jar in a warm place.

5 After about two days, a tiny root pushes through the bean's hard outer skin.

The bean contains the food that the new seedling needs to grow.

Add water to keep the paper moist.

Now that the new plant has leaves, it can make its own food (see page 23).

6 Over the next two days, the root grows downward, and a shoot starts to push its way up out of the bean.

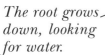

The shoot grows up, looking for light.

Tiny roots grow from the main root.

The root grows down, looking for water.

7 The seedling grows quickly. After ten days, the shoot has become a leafy stem.

Sowing seeds
This farmer is scattering seeds in a field. If the conditions are right, the seeds will germinate and grow into new plants.

Seed needs

What causes a seed to begin to germinate? By growing your own seeds you will discover that if they have water, oxygen from the air, and warmth, they will soon start to grow into plants.

You will need:

Three deep saucers

Water

Bean seeds

Bowl of water

Paper towels

1 Soak the seeds in water overnight. Drain and rinse them.

2 Put several paper towels in each saucer.

Add a little water to this saucer each day to keep the seeds moist.

4 Sprinkle seeds onto the paper in all three saucers.

3 Pour enough water into the first saucer to moisten the paper towels.

5 Gently fill the second saucer with water. Make sure that the seeds are completely covered. Leave the third saucer dry.

Add water every day to this saucer as well.

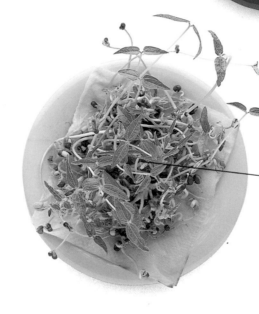

The dry seeds do not germinate at all.

6 Leave the saucers somewhere warm for about five days. The three sets of seeds will look quite different.

These seeds germinate and grow into young bean seedlings as they take in water and oxygen.

The seeds under water begin to germinate. But they do not have enough air, and growth soon stops.

Irrigation
Seeds need water to grow, and plants need water to stay alive. In areas where there is little rain, farmers must irrigate their crops to keep them from dying.

Too dark to grow?

Do seeds need light to germinate? You can find out by trying to grow some of your own seeds in the dark.

You will need:

Radish seeds

Lid or dish

Paper towels

Water

Large cup

1 Fold a moist paper towel and put it in the lid.

2 Gently sprinkle some seeds onto the paper.

3 Cover the seeds with the cup to keep out the light. Leave them in a warm place.

Check the seeds daily to see if they need more water. The paper towel should always be moist.

Growth after about six days

4 The seeds germinate and begin to grow, even though they are in the dark. But the seedlings will now need light to continue growing.

Spring bulbs
Bulbs are planted in holes in the soil. Their roots grow deep down into the earth before the first shoots appear in search of light.

Too cold to grow?

Why is it that plants never grow on cold, snowy mountaintops? You can find out by trying to grow seeds in the cold.

You will need:

Radish seeds

Lid or dish

Paper towels

Water

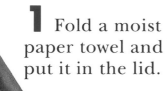

1 Fold a moist paper towel and put it in the lid.

2 Gently sprinkle some seeds onto the paper.

Make sure you keep the seeds moist.

3 Put the seeds in the refrigerator. Leave them for a few days.

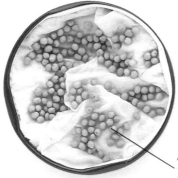

4 The cold seeds do not germinate. They need warmth to do so.

The seeds look just the same as when you put them in the refrigerator.

Icy wasteland

There are some areas of Antarctica that have no plant life. It is too cold all year round for plants to grow.

Plant maze

Plants need light to grow. They'll even find their way through a maze to get the light they need. Plants use light to make food once the food stored in their seeds has been used up.

You will need:

Two pieces of cardboard

Scissors

Pot of soil

Cardboard box

Water

Bean seed (soaked overnight)

1 Cut a rectangular hole in one end of the box.

2 Cut a rectangular hole in each piece of cardboard.

3 Plant the bean in the pot of soil. Water it well.

4 Stand the box upright and insert a cardboard shelf a third of the way up. Put the pot in the bottom of the box.

The hole in the cardboard should be on the side opposite the pot.

After four or five days the seedling has grown toward the light coming down through the hole.

5 Put the lid on the box and stand it in a light, warm place. Keep the bean moist.

Again, the opening in the cardboard should be on the side opposite the seedling.

6 When the seedling has grown through the first hole, insert the second shelf.

7 The seedling changes direction again. It grows through the second hole in the maze and toward the light.

Tall trees
Trees in a forest can grow to a great height. In their effort to get enough light, they may turn and bend as they grow.

Brilliant bean

Can a seed tell the difference between up and down? Turn some growing beans upside down to see how they are affected by gravity.

You will need:

Water

Paper towels

Bowl of water

Glass jar with lid

Two string bean seeds

The roots turn so that they continue to grow down. They are pulled down by gravity.

It does not matter which way the beans are pointing.

Make sure you keep the paper moist.

1 Soak the beans overnight. Crumple up some moist paper towels and put them in the jar. Add the beans.

2 After three or four days, roots start to grow down. A shoot pushes its way out of the bean.

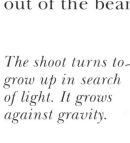

The shoot turns to grow up in search of light. It grows against gravity.

3 When the roots are about 3 cm (1 inch) long, screw the lid firmly on the jar and turn it upside down.

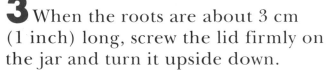

4 Three to four days later, the roots and shoots have changed direction.

Clever carrot

When you eat a carrot, you are actually eating the root of a carrot plant. You can grow a new carrot plant from a cut piece of carrot root.

You will need:

Young raw carrot

Knife

Saucer   Water

1 ⚠️ Ask an adult to cut off the top 3 cm (1 in.) of the carrot.

Add more water when the level falls.

2 Put the carrot top in a saucer and add some water. Keep the saucer in a warm, light place for a week.

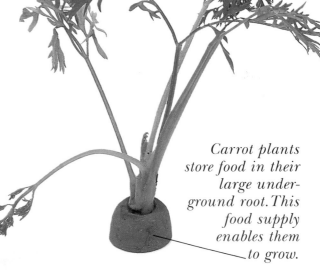

Carrot plants store food in their large underground root. This food supply enables them to grow.

3 The carrot top grows new leaves! You can also grow parsnips, beets, and turnips this way.

Plants from cuttings

Do new plants only grow from seeds? You can find out by taking a "cutting"—a small piece of a plant that can produce its own roots and grow into a whole new plant.

You will need:

Rubber band

Shears

Fully grown geranium plant

Pot of moist soil

Clear plastic bag

Leaf joint

1 ⚠ Find a strong young shoot without any flowers. Ask an adult to cut it off below a leaf joint.

Remove the lower leaves from the shoot before planting.

The shoot should be about 7.5cm (3in.) long.

2 Make a hole in the moist soil and plant the cutting in it.

Remove the bag when the cutting begins to grow. You will now need to water it regularly.

Secure the bag with a rubber band.

3 Put the bag over the cutting. Leave the pot in a warm place, out of direct sunlight.

The cutting grows its own roots. These take up water and minerals from the soil.

4 The cutting grows into a new geranium plant. This takes about six weeks.

Spreading strawberries

Strawberry plants can also make new plants without using seeds. Each parent plant grows special stems called "runners."

You will need:

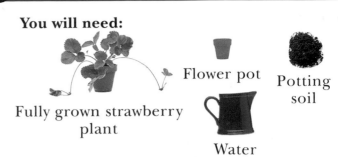

Fully grown strawberry plant

Flower pot

Potting soil

Water

1 Carefully fill the flower pot with soil.

Runner

Plantlet

2 Find a runner on the fully grown strawberry plant that has plantlets along it. Plant one of the plantlets in the pot. Water it well.

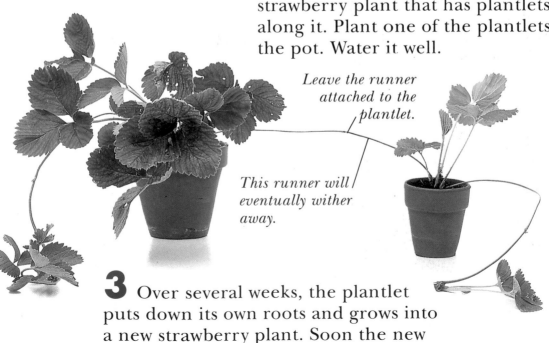

Leave the runner attached to the plantlet.

This runner will eventually wither away.

3 Over several weeks, the plantlet puts down its own roots and grows into a new strawberry plant. Soon the new plant sends out its own runners.

Root power

Plants send roots down through the soil to search for the water they need to live and grow. The roots also draw up minerals that help the plants grow. Roots are very strong. They can push their way through hard ground in their search for water and can even break things.

You will need:

Half an eggshell

Eggcup

Water

Potting soil

Marigold seeds

Saucer

Spoon

1 Carefully fill half an eggshell with soil.

2 Put the eggshell in the eggcup. Sprinkle the seeds over the soil.

4 Keep the eggshell in a warm, light place. Water the soil lightly every day.

Be careful not to overwater.

3 Put the eggcup on the saucer. Cover the seeds with a little soil.

5 The seeds germinate after a few days and shoots appear. Allow them to grow.

6 About five weeks later, the eggshell begins to crack. The roots of the marigold plants break through the eggshell.

The roots continue to grow in their search for more water and minerals for the growing plants.

Stone breakers
The pavement around trees is often lifted or even cracked. The roots of the trees are so strong that they can push up under the pavement and damage it.

Thirsty flower

How much water does a plant need to stay fresh and alive? By watering a flower with colored water you will see how plants take in water through their stems.

You will need:

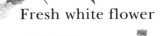

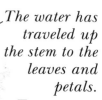

Narrow vase of water

Fresh white flower

Cooking oil

Food coloring

Rubber band

1 Add several drops of food coloring to the vase of water.

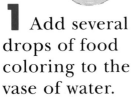

2 Gently pour the oil onto the water. Put the rubber band around the vase.

The oil floats on top of the water. It keeps any water from escaping into the air.

3 Put the flower in the vase. Move the rubber band so that it marks the top of the oil.

The water has traveled up the stem to the leaves and petals.

4 Leave the flower in a warm place for about two days.

The flower has taken in this much water.

Desert plants
Cacti can survive in dry deserts because they store water in their thick stems.

Bubbling plant

How do green plants make the food they need to grow? This experiment shows you that during the day green plants take in water and carbon dioxide and use sunlight to change them into food. This process is called "photosynthesis."

You will need:

Bowl of water

Water

Index card

Pondweed

Jar

1 Put the pondweed in the jar. Fill the jar with water.

Fill the jar to the top.

Make sure no air gets into the jar.

2 Hold the card over the top of the jar. Turn the jar over and submerge it in the bowl of water. Remove the card.

The bubbles are oxygen that forms when water and carbon dioxide (which is in air or water) are changed into food.

3 Put the jar where it will get plenty of light.

4 Bubbles appear on the leaves of the pondweed and rise to the top of the jar.

Indoor garden

You can make your own indoor garden in a plastic or glass jar. Your plants will have everything they need to live and grow inside the jar.

You will need:

Large jar with lid

Spoon

Small pebbles

Crushed charcoal

Potting soil

Spray bottle

Small plants

The pebbles help to drain the compost.

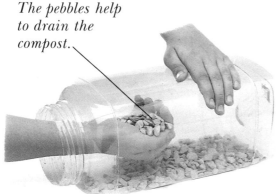

1 Lay the jar on its side. Cover the bottom with a layer of pebbles.

The charcoal keeps the water pure.

2 Next, cover the pebbles with a layer of charcoal.

3 Using the spoon, add a layer of soil.

4 Make holes in the soil and put a plant in each one. Press down firmly around each plant.

5 When everything is in place, spray two or three squirts of water over the plants.

If there are no drops of water on the inside of your jar the next day, spray more water inside.

If water drops completely cover the inside of the jar, leave it open for a day.

The plants have the water, air, light, and warmth they need to grow.

6 Put the lid on and leave your indoor garden in a warm, light place, out of direct sunlight.

Growing under glass

Plants grow well in greenhouses. The glass walls shelter the plants from the cold, but allow the sun's rays to provide them with the light and warmth they need to grow.

Yeast feast

Yeast is a very simple kind of organism called a "fungus." Fungi cannot make their own food, like green plants can, so they need to be fed. By giving yeast some sugar, you can make it inflate a balloon!

You will need:

 Balloon

 150 ml (half cup) warm water

 Narrow-necked bottle

 Three teaspoons of yeast

Two teaspoons of sugar

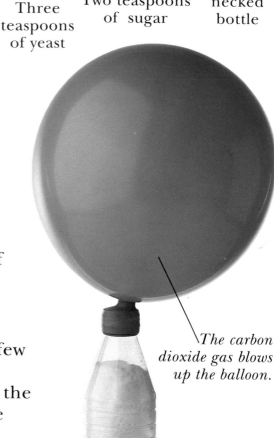

1 Put the yeast and sugar into the bottle. Gently pour in the warm water.

2 Put the neck of the balloon over the bottle.

3 Over the next few hours, the balloon slowly inflates and the liquid in the bottle becomes foamy.

The carbon dioxide gas blows up the balloon.

As the yeast feeds on the sugar, it produces bubbles of carbon dioxide.

Breadmaking
Yeast is used to make bread. Carbon dioxide gas, from yeast mixed with sugar, makes the dough rise before it is baked.

Spore print

Fungi, such as mushrooms, do not have seeds, so how do they grow? You can make some prints to see how "spores" drop from mushrooms. The spores float through the air before they land and grow into new mushrooms.

Flat mushrooms with dark undersides

Paper

1 Remove the stalks and place the mushrooms flat side down on the paper. Leave them for a day or two.

The patterns are made by tiny, dustlike spores that fall from the bottom of each mushroom cap.

2 Carefully lift the mushrooms. Each one has produced a pattern of dark powder on the paper.

Puffing plant
Puffballs are also fungi. They release clouds of spores when rain falls on them. These spores are then carried through the air and may grow into new puffballs where they land.

Magic mold

Mold is another kind of fungus. It grows where mold spores in the air land and find food, moisture, and warmth.

You will need:

Water

Antiseptic disinfectant

Flat plastic or glass dish

Plastic wrap

Three pieces of bread

1 You will need two pieces of fresh bread and one piece of stale bread.

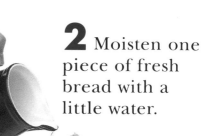

2 Moisten one piece of fresh bread with a little water.

3 ⚠ Ask an adult to pour a little disinfectant over the second piece of fresh bread.

Place the two pieces of bread as far apart as possible.

Keep the dry piece of bread outside.

4 Put the two wet pieces of bread in the dish. Cover the dish with plastic wrap and leave it in a warm place for several days.

Dry bread

Disinfected bread

Moist bread

5 After three days, mold begins to grow on the moist piece of bread. The dry bread and bread with disinfectant have no mold.

6 A few days later, the mold on the moist bread has grown quickly! What does the other bread look like?

The disinfectant kills the spores so no mold grows.

New mold spores

Mold has started to grow where there was a little moisture left in the stale bread.

Moisture and warmth help the mold feed on the bread so that the mold grows.

Picture credits
(Abbreviation key: B=below, C=center, L=left, R=right, T=top)

The Anthony Blake Photo Library/ Gerrit Buntrock: 9BL; J. Allan Cash Limited: 26BL; Bruce Coleman Limited/Gene Ahrens: 7TR; Pete Gardner: 6CR, 6BL, 7CL; Robert Harding Picture Library: 25BR; The Image Bank: 11BR, 22BL; Oxford Scientific Films/Michael Ogden: 27BL;

Pete Gardner: 21BL; Photos Horticultural/ Michael & Lois Warren: 12BR; Science Photo Library/European Space Agency: 6TL; Seaphot Limited/ Planet Earth Pictures: 13BR; Spectrum Colour Library: 15BR

Picture research Paula Cassidy and Rupert Thomas

Production Louise Barratt

Dorling Kindersley would like to thank Claire Gillard for editorial assistance; Mrs Bradbury, the staff and children of Allfarthing Junior School, Wandsworth, especially Idris Anjary, Billy Arthur, Tom Blyth, Miriam Habtesellasse, Ben Hedley, Thomas Hutchings, Mark Macleod, Anna Rimoldi, and Alice Watling; Tom Armstrong.